The Homewood

Surrey

Neil Bingham

National Trust

McDowell+Benedetti

34-35 Hatton Garden London EC1N 8DX United Kingdom
telephone 020 3475 7500   www.McDowellBenedetti.com

Above The garden front
in 2010

Right The garden front in
1993. The principal rooms
are on the first floor

TAILORED TO FIT

THE HOMEWOOD, near Esher, Surrey, is the sizable country villa designed and lived in by the architect Patrick Gwynne. He created the house for his family – his father, mother, sister and himself – and completed it in the early summer of 1938.

However, the Gwynnes lived together here for only a little over a year. When the Second World War broke out in the autumn of 1939, Commander Gywnne was forced out of retirement and re-entered the Royal Navy. Patrick joined the Royal Air Force, and his sister Noreen (known as Babs) joined the Women's Royal Naval Service.

During the war, when the house was let out to tenants, both parents died. Patrick and Babs returned to The Homewood in 1945; but Babs soon married and moved out, while Patrick remained. Here he lived, had his architectural office, tended the ten-acre garden and entertained. Until his death in May 2003, The Homewood was the focus of Patrick Gwynne's life, both personal and architectural. His friend, the architect Sir Denys Lasdun, observed that The Homewood was 'the great love of Patrick's life'.

Although Gwynne had begun to design the house in 1937, when he was only 24 years old, The Homewood was an extremely mature architectural *tour de force*. Having worked in the office of the cutting-edge modern architect Wells Coates, and travelled on the Continent looking at new buildings, Gwynne produced a highly sophisticated example of the early Modern Movement style, individualistic and luxurious.

The Homewood may be likened to an exquisitely tailored Savile Row suit. Gwynne designed the fabric and guided expert makers in executing the fine details. Then, over the next six decades that he lived in the house, he replaced those patches which had worn thin, while keeping it fashionably up-to-date. The Homewood developed and flourished with the architect's style, becoming an experimental showcase for his other architectural projects, which were mainly one-off houses for affluent clients, but also included a series of restaurants, as well as the Theatre Royal, York.

The uniqueness of The Homewood is that in the accumulation of design and details, of house and garden, and in the furnishings – most of them designed by Gwynne – we recognise a progression through the very best of the Modern Movement style in Great Britain.

Above Patrick Gwynne photographed by Anthony Buckley in 1939 – shortly after he had finished building The Homewood

Left A distant view from the garden

Below The old Homewood, the Victorian villa that Gwynne persuaded his parents to replace

Opposite The building that converted Gwynne to Modernism – Amyas Connell's High & Over, which was one of the first Modern Movement houses to be built in Britain

Patrick Gwynne was born in Portchester, Hampshire, in 1913. His father, Commander Alban Gwynne, was stationed with the Royal Navy in nearby Portsmouth, as officer-in-charge of the submarine mine school. His parents had met most romantically in Istanbul (then Constantinople), where the Commander was stationed and Ruby Bond just passing through on her return to England from India, where she had been born and raised.

A year after his birth, Patrick's parents moved to Esher, which was conveniently located on the railway line between Portsmouth and London. They first rented, then bought 'Homewood', a large Victorian house sited close to the A3 Portsmouth Road (now the A307) on the very property where The Homewood was to be built nearly 25 years later. Patrick's sister Babs was born soon after the move.

The house was often filled with friends, guests and, when times were tight financially, with lodgers. One such resident, in the early 1920s, was no less than Beatrice, Infanta of Spain, who rented part of the house to be close to her sons, who were boarding nearby at Sandroyd prepatory school in Cobham, which Patrick also attended. As a result, the young Patrick found himself meeting the Infanta's flamboyant sister, Queen Marie of Romania, who loved the garden. Other royal visitors were the Infanta's aunt, Queen Alexandra, and cousin, the dashing Edward, Prince of Wales, whom Patrick spied on as he strolled through the grounds with his latest girlfriend, Mrs Dudley Ward.

Between 1927 and 1930, Patrick attended Harrow School. It was during this period that he discovered Modern architecture. A favourite pastime was drawing, and on one occasion his mother picked him up from Harrow for a day-trip sketching, and they found themselves motoring into Amersham, Buckinghamshire. There they discovered the newly completed High & Over, one of the earliest, largest and most startling modern houses in Britain, designed by the architect Amyas Connell. As Patrick said of that moment, it 'sold me Modern'.

Above Le Corbusier's
Haus 13 on the
Weissenhofsiedlung
estate in Stuttgart

Right 'Shipwrights' in
Benfleet, Essex, where
Gwynne supervised building
work for Wells Coates

Opposite Le Corbusier's Villa
Savoye, near Paris, the key
source for The Homewood

GWYNNE AND THE EMERGING MODERN MOVEMENT

England had been slow to take up the new Modernism in architecture which had been gaining momentum during the 1920s on the Continent, especially in Germany, the Netherlands and France. Characterised by plain façades and interiors, usually flat-roofed with large windows and white rendering on the exterior, the aesthetic of Modernism was considered progressive and in touch with the new machine age of motor cars and aeroplanes.

When Gwynne first became excited by Modernism, in the late 1920s, it was mainly though illustrations in books and magazines.
On prize-giving day at Harrow, he always picked out the architectural books, and even then, in his teens, subscribed to the *Architectural Review*, which was an influential advocate of Modernism. But when the moment came for him to article to an architect, his father arranged for him to work for a traditional architect, John Coleridge of Coleridge & Jennings, who had been a pupil of Sir Edwin Lutyens. Although he spent two years 'plodding away on sub-Lutyens houses', as Gwynne dryly put it, he toured with a friend looking at the new architecture in Germany.

Gwynne left Coleridge's office after two years, having learnt the basics of draughtsmanship, took his Intermediate exams with the Royal Institute of British Architects, and then set about looking for a modern architectural practice to join. It was 1934, and the previous year Mendelsohn had moved to England from Berlin to escape the Nazi regime. Gwynne approached his architectural hero for a job, but was disappointed. Instead, he found a place in the office of Wells Coates, a leading light of British Modernism. Wells Coates was to shape Gwynne's view of Modernism.

Having just completed his most famous building, Lawn Road Flats, a large concrete block of 'minimal' flats in Hampstead, Wells Coates asked Gwynne to assist him in designing some of the built-in furniture for his latest large project, Embassy Court, Brighton. Then Gwynne received his biggest job, supervising the design and building of 'Shipwrights' in Benfleet, Essex, a weekend house overlooking the Thames estuary.

Gwynne left Coates's office in early 1937, conversant in Modern Movement design, an exceptionally talented architect, 24 years old, and eager to design his family's new home.

BUILDING THE HOMEWOOD

Patrick was very fortunate to have such indulgent and loving parents, who entrusted their young son with building their new home, and especially in such a Modern style. Not that they had much choice, he used to joke: 'I badgered and sold them my ideas from breakfast to dinner.' The old Victorian house was cramped and noisy, and so close to the road that 'the crockery bounced on the table'. Having inherited ancestral property in the Welsh harbour town of Aberaeron, Commander Gwynne sold it and used the money to build The Homewood.

Top The bedroom wing takes shape

Above The south front under construction. The building cost £10,500, leading Gwynne's father to describe it ruefully as 'the Temple of Costly Experience'

Opposite Stefan Knapp's enamel panels on the south front adopt the 1ft 8in x 4ft module, on which the whole design of The Homewood is based

Design

The Gwynnes chose a site on a raised area of their garden, facing south down its full length. Patrick began designing the house in April 1937. It was completed in little more than a year. To speed the operation, he made the detailed drawings while the house was under construction.

The plan is a highly articulated division of the three main functions of domestic life: the living area, sleeping quarters and services. The principal rooms are on the upper of the two storeys, taking advantage of the views. There are two wings, lying at right-angles to one another, joined by a square block housing the main entrance hall and central staircase. The longer wing, with a double tapering on its inward elevation, accommodates the bedrooms for family and guests; the L-shaped wing contains the expansive living and dining rooms for the family on the principal front, with the kitchen and staff quarters at the rear.

The house is based on Gwynne's own system of proportion: the vertical unit is 1ft 8in, the horizontal 4ft. Everything is a mathematical variation on this theme. This rational aesthetic gives the garden front its harmonious beauty. Each of the five bays is 12ft wide, ie 3 x 4ft.

Gwynne's design was inspired by several sources. In appearance, the master-bedroom section of The Homewood is similar to 'Shipwrights', the house designed by Wells Coates which Gwynne had supervised. And, without doubt, the houses of Le Corbusier were a major influence: the one at Weissenhofsiedlung, which Gwynne had visited, and that most famous of all Modern houses, the Villa Savoye at Poissy, just outside Paris. The long band of windows on the bedroom wing, balanced upon slender columns, is very Corbusian, although Gwynne added the vertical touches of the two large balconies, which he described as having pulled-out pieces of concrete like drawers.

Construction

Gwynne also adhered to the Modern method of construction and proportion. The Homewood has a reinforced concrete structure comprising supporting columns, first floor slab, internal columns and roof slab, and is variously exposed or clad in brick, render and paint. Wells Coates was instrumental in supplying reliable contractors and builders who were familiar with the latest techniques in construction like Felix Samuely, the structural engineer. Gwynne's friend Leslie Bilsby, with many connections in the furniture trade, acted as the consultant for all the major cabinetmaking.

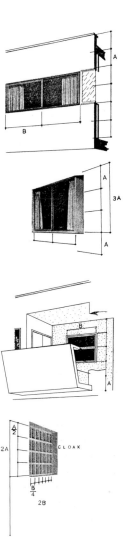

Above Gwynne's designs for the windows and openings, showing the vertical (A) and horizontal (B) units from which they are composed

Above Patrick Gwynne in RAF uniform during the Second World War

Right The Entrance Hall in 1939. The Gwynnes were avid tennis players

Opposite The Living Room in 1939. Music and dancing were central to life at The Homewood – hence the piano in the foreground, on which Gwynne's friend, the concert pianist Geoffrey Rand, would play

LIFE AT THE HOMEWOOD

The Gwynne family celebrated the completion of The Homewood with a party in July 1938. Pimms was followed by dinner on the terrace. It was the beginning of a year of entertainment. There was lots of tennis, played on the court down the garden. And dancing. 'We danced like mad,' recalled Gwynne, who had designed a sprung floor for the Living Room and built in a gramophone player for just such a purpose.

But when war was declared in 1939, life at The Homewood inevitably changed. Commander Gwynne, Patrick and Babs all left to enter the armed forces. With the house too large for her, Mrs Gwynne dismissed the staff – cook, housemaid and parlourmaid – keeping only the gardener, Whittle, and moved to a cottage in the grounds. The Homewood was let for a year to Robert Lutyens, son of the architect Sir Edwin Lutyens. Another tenant was the Chilean ambassador.

In 1942, both Commander and Mrs Gwynne died. When Patrick and Babs returned in 1945 at the end of the war, they moved back into The Homewood. Babs did not stay long, getting married and moving with her husband – first to the studio cottage, then to Essex. And so Patrick stayed on, at first assisted by a live-in housekeeper. For the next 58 years he maintained, refined and thoroughly enjoyed his house.

Getting back on his feet after the war, Gwynne converted his father's study into his own and changed his parents' bedroom into his architectural office, where at times three people worked. The house came alive again. Friends stayed, architectural students visited. And there were parties. Over the years, Gwynne made new friends, mostly in the arts. Many were clients:

the actor Jack Hawkins; Hollywood star Laurence Harvey and his wife, the model Paulene Stone; and the concert pianist Clifford Curzon.

Yet, for all this entertaining, Gwynne lived a disciplined and private life: discriminating, elegant and gentlemanly, and very single-minded. The Homewood is a reflection of Gwynne's personality.

CATERING FOR THE NATION

'Mine is a small practice and the works... have been mainly divided between private houses of a fairly luxurious standard designed for individual clients and large works mostly connected with the catering trade. I have been sought out by clients who wanted an unusual solution in the modern manner and where attention to detail was considered important.'

PATRICK GWYNNE

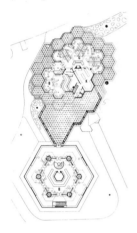

Above Plan of the hexagonal
Serpentine restaurant in
Hyde Park, which was
designed by Gwynne in
1963 and extended in
1965. It was demolished
in 1989

Opposite The Dell
restaurant in Hyde Park.
Designed by Gwynne in
1965

Right The Crescent
restaurant at the Festival
of Britain

After the war, Gwynne slowly returned to private practice, using The Homewood as his office and showcase. Preferring to work independently, he took on assistants only when he had larger projects. But that was later. At first, with post-war restrictions on private development, Gwynne

turned his hand to small jobs: a shoe shop in Catford, south London, which was so chic that it should have been on Bond Street; a gramophone shop in London's West End; a restaurant, the Ox on the Roof, in the King's Road.

His big break came in 1950, when he won the competition to build The Crescent restaurant in the Festival Gardens on London's Battersea Park for the Festival of Britain of 1951. It was reputedly the largest restaurant in Europe at the time, a building which captured both the Festival and Gwynne's light-heartedness. Behind its Big Top atmosphere there was much modern thought, brilliantly engineered by Felix Samuely, the engineer for the Festival's Skylon and The Homewood.

The caterer for The Crescent was Charles Forte (later Lord Forte), who was just beginning to build up his catering and hotel empire. In 1964 and 1965, Forte became a client for the two restaurants which Gwynne designed in Hyde Park. The first, called The Serpentine, was a series of interlocking six-sided blocks and towers, with raking glass walls, connected to a hexagonal section under a roof of giant mushrooming concrete umbrellas. Although, sadly, it was demolished in 1989, the other restaurant, The Dell, survives like an oversized pond lily floating above the eastern end of the waters of the Serpentine.

Above 115 Blackheath Park, London. Designed in 1949 for Gwynne's friend Leslie Bilsby, who advised on the cabinetwork for The Homewood

Right Another house in the woods: Grovewood in Sunningdale, Berkshire. Gwynne was a master at setting his houses in the landscape

Opposite The entrance hall of Witley Park, Surrey

Columns which spread like mushrooms were also a feature of Gwynne's Theatre Royal in York, from 1967. Having retained the theatre's late Victorian Gothic brick and stone façade, and refitted the auditorium, Gwynne added a new wing which contains the foyer, bar and restaurant, brilliantly illuminated and seen from the street at night through great sheets of plate-glass walling.

Through a school friend, the actor Hugh Latimer, Gwynne was meeting other actors. One was Jack Hawkins, for whose mother he built a house in Bournemouth in 1958, his first house since The Homewood twenty years earlier. More than a dozen one-off houses followed, all in London or the Home Counties. There were, as well, several major house conversions like that in Hampstead for Laurence Harvey, in which the architect tried to create a residence 'that might be in Beverly Hills'. Gwynne also designed and built a doctor's surgery in Henley-on-Thames, with a radiating plan; two octagonal-shaped motorway service areas at Burtonwood, Cheshire, on the M62 between Manchester and Liverpool; and an apartment block at St Paul's Bay on the island of Malta which has long balconies similar to those on The Homewood.

In Leslie Bilsby, the friend who had assisted him on the interior fittings and furnishings of The Homewood, Gwynne found a client who appreciated his avant-garde Modernism. In 1949 Gwynne radically altered a bombed-out Victorian house in Blackheath, south London, for the Bilsby family. Then in 1969, Bilsby, now a successful property dealer, commissioned Gwynne to build the most astonishing new house on Blackheath Park, with dark sleek façades of black slate and bronze-tinted glazing. And because Bilsby loved his parties to be intimate, Gwynne made every

room in the house the same size, and five-sided. Ten years later, Bilsby asked Gwynne to design yet another house for him, also in Blackheath, but this time with a plan of three linked octagons.

Gwynne's largest house was for the department store owner Gerald Bentall. Slightly larger than The Homewood, Witley Park in Surrey, is a lavish, modern country house on an historic estate. Here, as with all of Gwynne's other houses and conversions, it is possible to recognise elements of The Homewood: similar lighting features, built-in and free-standing furniture, a spectacular staircase, textured wall-coverings and many personal details which make Patrick Gwynne's buildings so ingenious and beautiful.

Above Design for the servery between the kitchen and dining room of 115 Blackheath Park

Below The Landing and top of the spiral staircase

Opposite The foot of the spiral staircase

The Entrance Hall

The front door is beneath the car-port canopy, which is raised upon piloti columns and covers the circular driveway. The door is surrounded by square glass blocks; from within the Entrance Hall, this dramatically encases the door in light, while helping the plants to grow in the sunken floor troughs on either side. The passage on the left leads to the Study (see p.28).

To the right of the entrance, at the far end, is the double-door to the terrace and garden. The green terrazzo bench and planter were designed by Gwynne, as was the double-light wall fitting,

around 1962. A glazed screen gives views to the terrace and garden beyond. The light switches are German with luminous rockers, original to the house. The walls are lined with simulated grass wall-covering, made of plastic, which Gwynne used to replace and replicate the original Japanese grass cloth, which had worn out.

Furniture

The telephone table mounted on the wall, by Gwynne from the 1950s, has tambour doors, which slide back to reveal shelves for telephone directories. The orange upholstered chair is Danish, by France & Son, and the metal three-leg mesh 'Nagasaki' chair was designed by Mathieu Mategot, both purchased by Gwynne in the 1950s.

The Central Staircase and Landing

The striking central spiral staircase is made of concrete with a terrazzo finish. A large sunken uplighter illuminates the staircase from its base. The top landing is a spacious open room, filling the first floor of the central block of the house. Glazed front and rear, it links the bedroom and living wings to either side. Commander Gwynne purchased the delicate antique Bristol blue and white glass chandelier, and although many visitors found it incongruous in such a modern house, Patrick Gwynne always thought it 'perfect for the situation'.

The abstract mural on the curved wall was drawn in coloured wax crayon on brown lining paper by an assistant of the artist Peter Thompson and was originally intended to be only temporary. The wall to the living wing is covered in tinted glass, and the pair of doors to the main living space are padded in white leather.

Top The front door is framed
by a glass-brick wall

Above The Entrance Hall
in 1993

17

The Living Room

The south-facing side of the room is a dramatic wall of glass, giving a raised view down the length of the garden. There are three identical large windows: each divided into three horizontals, with the central section able to open, gliding effortlessly up on sash mechanisms which Gwynne imported from Germany. The Venetian blinds, attached to little motors, may be raised and lowered by the flick of a switch.

The opposite wall is a masterly piece of cabinetmaking, a series of built-in wall units, which were originally covered in a walnut veneer, but when this faded, Gwynne replaced it with the present Indian laurel. The tripartite arrangement echoes the windows. The outer sections have inset shelving for books and displaying objects, lit with hidden strip-lighting. The centre section is enclosed by sliding tambour doors; behind these are spaces for the drinks cabinet, hi-fi equipment and a serving hatch through to the Kitchen on the other side of this wall. Beneath the middle segment, convenient to the hatch, is a concealed built-in serving-table which Gwynne used for parties or buffets, pivoting it out from the wall and unfolding its single tubular metal leg.

The east end wall, remodelled in the 1960s, is covered in a brown Swedish fabric, overlaying fibreglass sheeting to dampen the acoustics of the room. The far end wall is of polished black Levanto marble, with fine red, white and green veining. A gas fireplace is cut neatly into it.

Furniture

Originally, the furniture was more light-weight, so that it could be easily pushed aside for dancing – the maple floor is sprung. Over the years, Gwynne altered, adapted and refurbished the furniture, designing many new pieces for the room to meet his changing needs and aesthetic.

The seating area in the corner near the window is where Gwynne used to relax most often, in the classic leather Eames lounge chair and matching ottoman, a gift from Paulene Stone, having belonged to her late husband, Laurence Harvey. It is grouped with a beige leatherette-covered couch with ebonised supports, designed by Gwynne in the 1960s. The couch is attached to the wall, but could be pivoted out so that the built-in projection screen could be raised and angled when Gwynne wanted to show his home movies. From around the same date are the coffee table, with its slender yew top and metal rod supports, the delicate standard reading lamp with a Shantung silk shade, and the low square red and black lacquered chest-of-drawers, all by Gwynne. Over the couch is a large drawing in dyes on paper by the artist Stefan Knapp.

Opposite The Living Room today

Below The Living Room in 1993

The Living Room

Furniture

Near the panelled wood wall are two more of Gwynne's designs from the 1960s. Wanting a place to work in the Living Room, he created this dual-purpose desk, originally in white leather, but later replaced with white vinyl, raised on interestingly shaped anodised aluminium legs. With its top down, it is a writing-table; when the top is removed, a drawing-table can be raised and tilted. A lamp unfolds from a channel in the desk surface. There is a pull-out drawer for a typewriter on one side, and another drawer for stationery and drawing instruments on the other. Beside it is a low black side-table designed to house sheet music. Between the television and the marble fireplace wall is a bronze sculpture,

entitled *The Japanese Actor*, by Oliffe Richmond, who was once an assistant to Henry Moore. The Bauhaus chair (designed by Marcel Breuer) behind the desk was one of the first originals imported to Britain. Disliking the chrome finish, Gwynne had it stove-enamelled in ivory.

Near the window, where they have been since The Homewood was completed, is a pair of *chaise-longues* by the Swedish designer Bruno Mathsson, covered by Gwynne in beaver lamb 'fur'. Between is a Gwynne-designed magazine table, made of American walnut on a brass frame, with a pull-out shelf for resting drinking cups.

Gwynne provided a space divider in the form of a bookcase, specially created to house his set of *Encyclopaedia Britannica*. Upon it rests a wooden abstract sculpture by the San Dominican artist Martinez. To its right is a long table, designed by Gwynne in the 1960s for the dual purpose of having a refectory-style surface to sit or work at combined with a specialised compartment to house a ciné film editor.

Grouped near the fireplace are two pieces original to the setting and both designed by Gwynne: the occasional table with a thick round glass top and rosewood frame, its legs lowered by three inches better to suit the large semicircular button-back sofa. Originally, the sofa was upholstered in blue fabric; when this wore out, Gwynne replaced it with the present imitation brown suede, while also lowering the back. There were once two matching tub chairs, but Gwynne substituted for these the white *chaise-longue* and matching chairs by the English designer William Plunkett.

The television cabinet was designed by the Danish firm Bang & Olufsen.

Above The bar in the living room swings out from the wall. Above and below are sliding doors that conceal a drinks cabinet, hi-fi and serving hatch. The Homewood is full of such ingenious touches

Right A folding screen separates the Living Room from the Dining Room beyond

Opposite The Living Room, with the Dining Room beyond. The fireplace wall is covered with Levanto marble

The Dining Room

The Dining Room lies at the far end of the Living Room and can be shut off by a folding screen door. The Living Room side of the screen was delicately painted with images of bamboo by Peter Thompson, an artist born and brought up in China; the side facing the Dining Room is decorated with stalks of sweet corn highlighted in gold leaf on a black background. Within the thickness of the wall is a recess for storing ciné equipment. The serving-end wall is wood-veneered with fitted drawers, cupboards and shelves for glasses. The door leads to the kitchen quarters. When Gwynne upgraded the serving alcove in the 1960s, he inserted the built-in warming plates and *bain-marie* and commissioned the artist Stefan Knapp to create the beautiful yet utilitarian splashback, which doubles as the serving hatch, in a pattern of gold and silver leaf enamel baked on steel.

Above The Dining Room side of the folding screen is decorated with stalks of sweet corn painted in gold

Right The Dining Room

Pictures

The four ancestral portraits were painted about 1810 by Mather Brown, an American artist who had settled in Britain in 1781. The older gentleman is the Rev. Alban Gwynne (1751–1819), and his companion is his second wife Susannah Jones (1754–1830), who together were responsible for transforming the small fishing port of Aberaeron, Wales, into a sizeable harbour, and hence creating the Gwynne family fortune. The young couple are the Rev. Alban Gwynne's son by his first marriage, Col. Alban Gwynne, and his wife, Mary Anne Vevers (1781–1837).

Furniture

In the left-hand corner of the room stands a Bechstein boudoir grand piano. The oval music cabinet with a rosewood top and maple tambour door is by Gwynne, from about 1960.

The round dining-room table is a marvellous dinner conversation-piece. Gwynne designed it in the early 1960s to replace the original table, which was in two separate rectangles, also designed by Gwynne. The base is formed of two equal aluminium spinnings with an internal steel framework. The top is grey-tinted glass sprayed black on the reverse; the trim edge is plated steel. Sunk in the centre of the table top is a circular

well with three hidden coloured lights; the control knobs for dimming and colour variations are at the host's fingertips. A perspex bowl for flowers can be inset in the well at a level so as not to interfere with guests' views; or the opening can be covered so that objects placed over it may be lit from below.

The set of dining-chairs, covered in white vinyl and called the Executive Chair, was designed in 1957 by the architect Eero Saarinen. Gwynne designed the elegant metal-framed side-table, with two glass-top surfaces, in the 1950s for additional serving space.

In the wall niche is a sculpture by Bridget McCrum.

The Balcony

Through a double pair of sliding doors is the Balcony, with a south- and west-facing aspect overlooking the pool. Gwynne designed the glass-top table, on a white stove-enamelled base in the 1960s, as well as the two sets of four aluminium plant containers.

The four mesh chairs were designed by Harry Bertoia in 1952.

Top The Balcony

Above The view from the Dining Room in 1993

Left Gwynne's Welsh ancestors, whose property in Aberaeron paid for the building of The Homewood. From left to right: The Rev. Alban Gwynne; his second wife, Susannah Jones; his son, Alban, and daughter-in-law, Mary Anne Vevers

The Kitchen extends along the rear of the house, behind the living area. It may be entered from the central staircase landing, or from the Dining Room, via a narrow servery. When the house was built, Gwynne designed the Kitchen in three sections with partition walls, one segment for the cook, the others for the maids, because, he said, they used to argue about their own territory in the old house.

Right The Kitchen as originally designed

The Kitchen

Gwynne changed most of the original kitchen fixtures and fittings, mainly between the late 1950s and early 1970s, making it better suited for a bachelor living and cooking on his own. A few of the fitments are original, sometimes just moved about. But the overall impression, with its rich brown painted and vinyl surfaces, is a transformation from the original.

Under the windows are the counter, sinks and lower cupboards. Still original are the spice rack, knife-holder and frosted glass washing-up alcoves. The opposite wall is fully built-in, using some of the units from the original kitchen, with a running line of high cupboards, shelving units and additional under-counter cupboards. The serving hatch to the Living Room is here too.

Overhead, Gwynne designed the suspended aluminium frame for hanging pots and pans, and the two long uplighters.

The island work counter in the centre of the kitchen, with a brown tiled surface and pull-out cutting boards, was a favourite design of Gwynne's, which he repeated in many of the houses he created. The round kitchen trolley is also by Gwynne.

A PASSIONATE COOK

Gwynne loved good food and fine wine, designing a menu with the same intensity as a building. He was a perfectionist, whether cooking an omelette or Lobster Thermidor, which was a particular favourite. He made his own bread, cakes, tarts, jams, ice-cream, sorbets and even pasta. His large collection of cookery books was heavily annotated where recipes were found wanting.

Left The Kitchen in 1993

The family bedrooms fill the first floor of the east wing. Very modern for the 1930s is the fact that much of the furniture was built-in, and that there were many bathrooms and WCs.

Above A Gwynne-designed ceiling light in a bedroom corridor

Right The Powder Room

The Bedrooms

When The Homewood was completed, there were five bedrooms, plus the master bedroom suite; but Gwynne reduced these to four in the 1950s, as he had originally intended. The bedroom which disappeared had been created for his grandmother, his mother's mother, who occupied it for a time when the whole family lived together.

From the staircase landing there are four openings grouped around the curved wall. A door leads into the master bedroom suite, originally for Gwynne's parents, but later converted to the architect's drawing office. At the time of Gwynne's death, with the help of the National Trust, he had just completed the process of turning this room back into the master suite.

From the landing to the left is a corridor which narrows to its far end, a reflection of the tapering side of this wing of the house. A long window overlooks the forecourt, while the glass blocks on the internal wall give light to the bathrooms. The two end bedrooms were for guests: a little one at the very end of the corridor, and the larger one with its own bathroom, dressing room and access to the balcony. The two doors on either side of the curved landing wall lead to the bedrooms for Patrick (on the left) and guests (on the right). They are almost mirror images of one another.

Furniture

Both rooms have their original cream leather single beds, suspended mahogany bedside tables and overhead shelf with hidden reading and uplights. The two sliding doors of the fitted wardrobes reveal, on one side, space for hanging clothes and tray storage, and on the other, an inset dressing-table with plate glass and vanity mirrors, wash-basin and top light. Side doors lead on to balconies.

Patrick furnished his room with an under-window suspended wall unit with sliding tambour doors, a bentwood chair covered in beaver wool to simulate fur, and a table, both by Bruno Mathsson and original to the house.

Patrick's Bathroom

The bathroom, side-lit through glass blocks, has blue-grey mosaic tiling with a blue tub and wash-basin from the 1950s.

The Powder Room

Between the bedrooms is the Powder Room, designed at Babs's insistence, because she was tired of having to share her bedroom in their old Victorian house with arriving party guests. The little tiled shelf follows the convex curve of the wall and is inset with a pair of round mirrors on metal stalks. There are matching stools beneath. The wall is hung with hand-painted silk. The side walls are glass block. The rear wall has a wash-basin flanked by two full-length mirrors.

Return to the Top Landing and walk down the stairs to the Entrance Hall.

Left The bathrooms were placed in the centre of the bedroom wing and so depend on borrowed light filtered through the glass-brick walls

Below Patrick's Bedroom

The WC and Flower Room
To the left of the entrance is a short corridor leading to the study. Behind the frosted-glass partition is a WC with a narrow wash-basin. The corridor leads past leads past the small Flower Room on the right, a space to cut and arrange garden flowers, with a sink, shelves for vases, and a door with direct access to the terrace.

The Study was originally Commander Gwynne's, placed so that visitors would not enter the main part of the house. Patrick turned it into his study-office, and in the 1960s transformed it to its present appearance. Here he worked, sketched and draughted, and received clients.

Furniture

The long desk is worthy of the bridge of a starship, raised up on a single angled metal leg which hides the telephone and electric wiring. Gwynne designed it to combine three functions: in the centre is a telephone exchange, to one side a drawing-table, to the other a desk surface. Overhead is a long lighting unit. Behind is a low drawer unit for filing. A sliding unit brings out the typewriter.

The circular table is contemporary with the desk, with little pull-out shelves for clients to set their drinks upon. In the corner, a white tubular chair and box table hang from the walls, which, like the small marble-top table, are all of Gwynne's design. Above hang three drawings by Henri Gaudier-Brzeska (1891–1915).

The Terrace

In the terrace lobby is a glass mosaic mural by Gwynne. The orange tiles form a plan of The Homewood. The black lines are lettering, very difficult to interpret: the short and wide lines read *The Homewood* and the thin ones *Patrick Gwynne*.

Right **The Study**

The terrace stretches the length of the garden side of The Homewood. Standing here affords a close view of the south façade and the six enormous squares (with squares within) which compose the upper elevation: the window of the connecting block; the three windows of the Living Room; and the westerly two made up of twelve enamel panels by the artist Stefan Knapp, from the late 1950s, ending with the framed openings of the balcony.

The oval ornamental pool was designed by and a gift of Sir Denys Lasdun – a colleague at the Wells Coates practice – as a gift to Patrick's parents. The large cast sculpture *Stalking Figure* is a replica of the original dated 1963, by Oliffe Richmond.

The terrazzo furniture, much of it built-in, is Gwynne's design. The suspended terrazzo bench is made for cushions to be placed on the seat and hung from the pegs on the brick wall. Tucked around the corner is the built-in barbecue, which is clad in riven slate offcuts, an idea suggested by Peter Thompson.

At the west end of the terrace are three small planting pools and the swimming pool,

ornamentally shaped and coloured with aquamarine tiles. These were designed by Gwynne in 1974.

The Service Wing

Leading off the Kitchen, with its own entrance near the garage, is the Service Wing containing a number of rooms originally occupied by staff. Before the Second World War, when The Homewood had just been completed, the Gwynnes employed three live-in women, almost always Welsh, as cook, housemaid and parlourmaid. Commander Gwynne also had a manservant with his own quarters on the ground floor. The room was later converted into changing rooms for the outdoor pool, sun-bed, jacuzzi and sauna.

The Garage

This occupies most of the ground floor of the Living Room wing. As each member of the Gwynne family had their own car, the garage needed to be large enough to house four cars. Gwynne's last car – a 1974 Aston Martin V8 series III – may be seen occasionally.

Above Relief on the exterior wall, by Angelo Biancini

Left The Terrace in Autumn, 2004

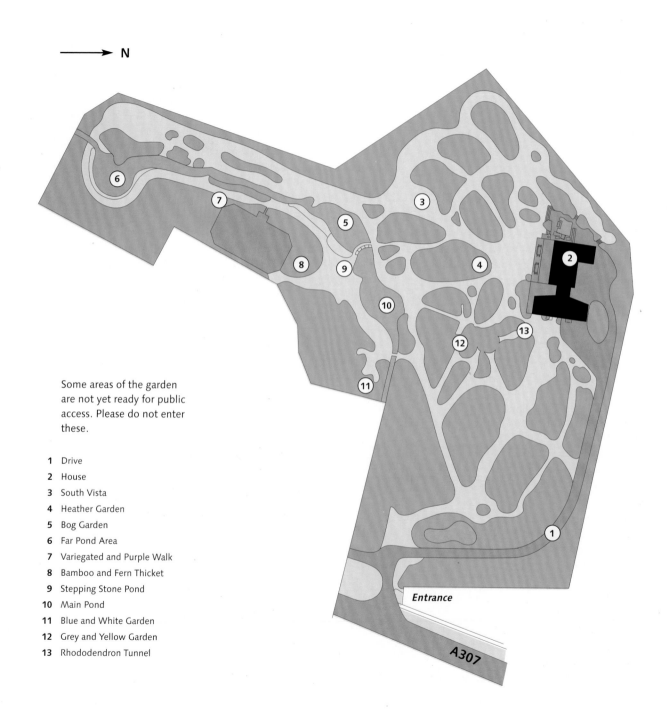

N

Some areas of the garden
are not yet ready for public
access. Please do not enter
these.

1 Drive
2 House
3 South Vista
4 Heather Garden
5 Bog Garden
6 Far Pond Area
7 Variegated and Purple Walk
8 Bamboo and Fern Thicket
9 Stepping Stone Pond
10 Main Pond
11 Blue and White Garden
12 Grey and Yellow Garden
13 Rhododendron Tunnel

Entrance

A307

THE GARDEN

Patrick Gwynne was keen to point out that the ten-acre setting of The Homewood was 'a woodland garden, not a park'. Lying in the midst of the woods of Esher Common, the garden is bisected by a stream, flowing to the nearby River Mole, from which Gwynne created a series of ponds. His father had been a skilled gardener, who surrounded their former house with luxurious bedding, lawns, shrubbery and trees. However, it was not until the 1960s that Patrick Gwynne began to create the landscape which we enjoy today, with the assistance of his close friends Raymond and Janet Menzies, who dealt with most aspects of the house and the landscaping of the garden. Highlights are the spring interest of rhododendrons and bluebells, and the autumn colours of Japanese maples.

As you approach from the entrance on the Portsmouth Road, the **drive** turns to the right with a sudden fine view of the bedroom wing of the house seen along the east vista and across the Drive Pond, an artificial pool from about 1970. Nearer the house, both sides of the drive are thick with rhododendrons and laurels.

The **south front of the house** was strategically placed to provide views over much of the garden. Overhanging the terrace are Japanese maples. Originally, there were great oaks and other trees crowding near the house, but these were removed and the vista to the main pond and the very long **south vista** created. There are many changing shades of purple and whites in the **heather garden**, which nestles in the beds at the approach to the vistas.

As you walk down the south vista, the birch trees on Esher Common rise to the west. These self-seeded after drought and fire in 1976. Gwynne also lost 53 of his own trees in the great

storm of 1987. Local heathers carpet the side of the path at its beginning. A copper beech, planted in March 2004, commemorates Patrick Gwynne, whose ashes are buried at its foot. A little further along is the **bog garden**, two islands in the stream planted with day-lilies, hostas and irises. Past the tennis court is the termination of the south vista, with a series of giant pines and views across the meadow of the **far pond area**.

Returning via the bamboo and fern thicket, you reach the **variegated and purple walks**, a medley of purple cherry trees (*Prunus cerasifera* 'Pissardii') and vegetation of mottled colouring. Passing through the tunnel of the **bamboo and fern thicket**, one emerges at the **stepping-stone pond**, followed by the wonderful giant rhubarb-like leaves of the *Gunnera manicata* in and around the **main pond**. Beneath the willow trees is the Portland stone sculpture *Eclipse*, by Bridget McCrum, 1999. Behind, across the **blue and white garden**, with its pattern of herringbone brick paving, rises a great Wellingtonia, the American sequoia.

After crossing the concrete bridge, the gentle rise of the York stone steps takes you amongst the **grey and yellow garden**, along the brick path and finally through the **rhododendron tunnel** back to the house.

Above View over red tulips on the terrace into the garden

Left Steps going down to the swimming pool and garden